# FUN DOUGH

# FUN DOUGH

## Over 100 salt dough projects for all the family

Brenda Porteous

DAVID PORTEOUS
CHUDLEIGH • DEVON

A CIP catalogue record for this book is available from the British library

ISBN 1 870586 01 8

Published by David Porteous
PO Box 5
Chudleigh
Newton Abbot
Devon TQ13 0YZ

Printed in Great Britain by
BPCC Paulton Books Limited

PUBLISHER'S NOTE
We hope you enjoy this book and making the items shown.
    If you would like to receive details of other David Porteous craft books please
write to the above address enclosing a stamped addressed envelope.

# Foreword

Making salt dough models and decorations really is a hobby for all the family and gives everyone a chance to develop their creative skills - or discover ones they did not know they had.

Very little is needed by way of tools and equipment, and all of the ingredients are already to be found in the kitchen.

Painting the models with acrylic paints is very easy, and the paints are readily available in art or stationery shops. A small selection of colours is all you require.

Above all, salt dough modelling should be fun, so don't worry if your first attempts are not quite as good as you would like because you will soon get the hang of things. Most times apparent 'failures' are turned into triumphs with the application of a little paint!

I hope the ideas shown in this book will give you lots of inspiration for things to make for yourself as well as gifts for others.

Last but not least, I would like to thank all the dough artists who have contributed to this book: Rachel Sargent, Val Sheldrake (who can be contacted on 0942 34068), Emily Brewer, Diane Clasper, Amanda Cooper, Christopher Bennett, Siân Brooks and Margaret Powell. The Artists' initials are shown next to each illustration.

# Contents

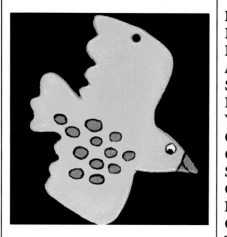

# Fun Dough: Baking and Painting

## THE BASIC RECIPE

2 level cups of plain flour
1 heaped cup of table salt
¾ cup of lukewarm water
1 tbsp of wallpaper paste
1 tbsp of vegetable oil

The recipe shown above is the one I have used for all the models in this book. After you have experimented with the dough you may find that you want to alter the proportions of the ingredients to suit yourself. Some dough artists use dough mixtures which exclude the wallpaper paste or the oil, or even both of them.

### Kneading

Blend the flour, salt and wallpaper paste together and then pour on the oil and water. If you have the good fortune to possess an electric mixer which also has a dough kneading attachment then this is the time to use it. If you are not so lucky, thoroughly stir the ingredients together in the bowl and then pour the mixture on to your work surface.

At this stage the dough may look rather dry, but after it has been kneaded for 10 or 15 minutes it should be firm but pliable. The dough should be reasonably firm so that the models keep their shape.

If the dough still appears to be dry after kneading for 15 minutes try kneading it a little longer. If this fails add a little more water.

Conversely, if the dough sticks to your hands add a little more flour.

### Storing

When you are satisfied with the consistency of the dough it should be kept covered, or in an airtight container, because it will dry very quickly if left uncovered. The dough can be kept in polythene bags but extreme care must be taken whenever young children are around because of the possible danger of suffocation.

The best results are obtained if the dough is kept in a cool place and used within a few days of making.

### Working with dough

The ideal work surface is the kitchen table because that ensures that you have sufficient room to spread your materials and tools in an orderly way. Very few tools are needed (see page 15) and half the fun is improvising and experimenting with everyday kitchen utensils — the garlic press is a good example.

I prefer to assemble the dough models on greaseproof paper and then carefully transfer them to a baking tray.

The dough is easy to shape and can be rolled flat like pastry, formed into sausage-shaped rolls or pinched into almost any shape. It can also be cut with a knife or snipped with scissors to form decorative patterns. Another way of decorating the surface is to impress it with a modelling tool or knife blade.

If the temperature in the kitchen is too high, or if your hands are too warm, the dough may become soft and difficult to work because it will not hold its shape.

### Joining the dough

The individual pieces which make up a dough model are very easily joined together by moistening the contact areas with a little water on a small paintbrush. The pieces are then gently pressed together. Quite elaborate models are built up in this very simple way.

For models which have a number of stages it is best to keep the earlier stages covered to prevent their becoming too dry for the later stages to adhere to them. If they do become dry it is possible to make a 'glue' from dough paste.

The dough paste is simply a small amount of salt dough which is made into a smooth paste by adding a little water and stirring. This mixture is then used to glue the pieces together.

## Hanging

For models which are to be wall decorations there are two choices of hanging style. The first is to simply make a hole near the top of the model by pushing a drinking straw through it. This makes a clean hole through which a ribbon can be threaded after baking.

The second style is to bend a piece of wire into a U shape and then press it into the top of the model to form a small loop. Brass or copper wire is ideal because it will not rust. Alternatively a paper clip can be used.

Always remember to insert the wire before baking.

## Air-drying

Models can be air-dried but it does take a long time. The advantage of this method is that it is the most economical and saves electricity and gas. It may take several weeks to dry a really thick model by this method.

Disadvantages are that there is a tendency for the base of the models to distort, and if the humidity is too high the salt absorbs moisture from the air and softens the dough.

However, some economies can be made by allowing the models to air-dry for a few days (I put mine on top of the central heating boiler) and then finishing them off in the oven for two or three hours. This method is better for thicker models, but the oven temperature should be low to begin with and gradually increased.

## Oven baking

Ovens may vary quite considerably and the following times and temperatures are guidelines only.

*Gas oven* baking times can be as short as half the baking time of an electric oven. This is because gas has a high moisture content which allows the surface moisture of the model to dry slowly but the inner moisture to dry more quickly.

Set the oven at its lowest temperature and bake the models for one hour with the oven door half-open. Bake for a further hour with the oven door quarter-open. Finally, bake for one hour with the oven door closed.

*Electric ovens* of all kinds are suitable, whether fan-assisted or not, but you may have to experiment with baking times to suit your particular oven.

The three methods you may wish to try are (i) *slow drying* at a constant low temperature, (ii) *medium drying* with a gradual increase in temperature, or (iii) *quick drying* at a high temperature.

*Slow drying* is probably the safest way of preventing the dough from rising or cracking. The oven temperature should be 75–80°C (170–190°F), or 50°C (130°F) for fan-assisted ovens. Bake for about 12 hours.

*Medium drying* is quicker but care must be taken that the models do not rise or crack at the higher temperatures. Bake for 1–2 hours at 75–90°C (170–200°F); then 1–2 hours at 100°C (210°F); then 1–2 hours at 125°C (260°F), and finally 1–2 hours at 150°C (300°F).

*Quick drying* is only really suitable for small models. Bake them for 2 or 3 hours at 110–120°C (230–250°F).

## Testing

The simplest way is to remove the baking tray from the oven and gently tap the model with your finger, both back and front. It should sound hollow. If it sounds dull it is still moist inside and should be placed back in the oven.

## Painting

The models are ready to be painted after baking.

In some cases you may wish to preserve a rustic appearance by simply applying a thin wash of colour in shades of brown. For other models you may wish to use bright, bold primary colours. Some models will look better in naturalistic colours. Acrylic paints provide the best solution for all of these approaches.

Acrylic paints are available in tubes and can easily be found in art shops and stationers. They are water soluble, non-toxic and odourless. The paint dries quickly and the brushes are very easily cleaned in water.

Because the paint dries quickly it is important not to let the paint dry on the brush, otherwise it becomes almost impossible to clean it.

Get into the habit of rinsing your brush when you have finished using a colour.

You need only a small selection of basic colours because you will be able to intermix them. Start with the primaries — red, yellow and blue. These can be mixed to form the secondary colours — orange (red plus yellow), green (yellow plus blue) and violet (red plus blue). Black or white can be added to any of these to darken or lighten them.

To create sepia effects I use burnt umber or burnt sienna, which I thin down with water and apply as a wash. If you thin the colour down too much don't worry because another wash can be added after the first is dry. If it looks too dark, quickly wipe it off with a clean, damp brush. This lightens it by letting the pale colour of the dough show through. This is also a useful technique for creating highlights, for example on the tips of leaves. Use a fairly stiff brush for wiping off the colour.

For gold effects I use Humbrol gold enamel paint. Carefully read the instructions on the can because this paint is flammable. Brushes must also be cleaned with white spirit.

You can buy ceramic palettes like the one shown on page 15, but an old ceramic plate or saucer is just as good. Ceramic palettes are better than plastic ones because the paint bonds to the plastic and it is impossible to totally remove it.

The best brushes for applying colour are synthetic ones because of their springy nature. I use Daler nylon or 'Daylon'.

For creating highlights I use a hog-hair Daler 'Bristlewhite' brush. Initially you will probably only need one medium size nylon brush, which is suitable for most purposes, a fine one for painting details and a hog-hair for highlighting.

**Varnishing**

All dough models must be varnished back and front after painting. The models will still absorb moisture from the air unless they are totally sealed with varnish.

I use polyurethane wood varnish, either matt or glossy depending upon the subject matter. Always follow the manufacturer's instructions and always use in well-ventilated areas.

**Tools**

The best tools of all, and the ones you will mostly use, are your fingers. However, there are some tasks which can only be done with special tools.

Creating hair, in the form of dough 'spaghetti', has to be done with either a garlic press or a clay gun. Clay guns are obtainable from pottery supply shops but they are also available from many shops which sell cake decorating accessories.

A range of pastry cutters speeds up the process of cutting leaves and flowers. The variety of shapes and sizes available is enormous.

A pointed skewer or modelling tool, in either wood or plastic, is very useful for delicate work

such as stalk indentations on fruit, or the centres of flowers.

The knife shown opposite is not only used for cutting and shaping the dough but also used for impressing patterns in the dough.

1. large metal pastry cutters
   (star, heart and leaf shapes)
2. small metal pastry cutters
   (flower and leaf shapes)
3. small craft knife
4. wooden skewer
5. hog-hair brushes
6. small nylon brush
7. medium 'Dalon' brush
8. garlic press
9. clay gun
10. kitchen knife
11. ceramic palette
12. polythene pastry cutters
13. acrylic paints

# Step-by-step: Sheep

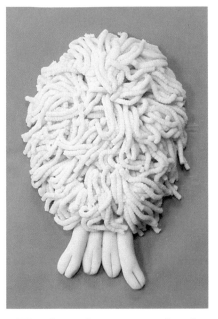

1 Make four small rolls for the legs. Snip one end of each roll with a pair of scissors to form the hooves. Place two rolls together to form the back legs, and then position the front legs slightly on top of the back legs.

For the base of the body roll out a small oval of dough and place it so that it overlaps the top of the legs. Remember to moisten the tops of the legs with a damp paintbrush before the body is put in place.

3 Starting at the bottom of the body, build up the fleece with the dough strands.

4 The fleece is now completed and the body is ready for the head to be positioned.

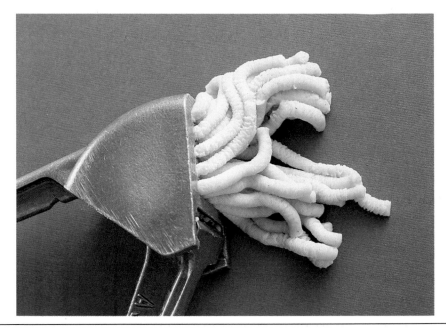

2 To make the sheep's fleece put a small ball of dough into a garlic press. Gently squeeze the press and trim off the strands of dough with a sharp knife.

5 To form the head, roll out a little dough and shape it into a triangle with rounded corners.

For the ears, take two small balls of dough and flatten them between finger and thumb to form an oval shape. Fold in half lengthways. Moisten the ears with a damp paintbrush and then gently apply them to the top two corners of the face. Moisten the back of the face and attach it to the body.

The whites of the eyes are two small balls of dough, which are moistened and positioned on the face. Two smaller balls of dough are then positioned to form the pupils.

Insert a paper clip into the top of the model to form a loop for hanging.

6 Check that the model is properly baked by tapping the back and front with your finger. It should make a hollow sound.

After baking, paint the legs, face and pupils of the eyes with black acrylic paint.

Leave the fleece unpainted.

7 When the paint is dry apply the varnish to both back and front to seal the model thoroughly.

The varnish also helps give a richer colour to the fleece.

# Step-by-step: Tree

1 Make a roll of dough and snip the top with a pair of scissors to form the branches.

Pinch the bottom of the roll to form the base of the trunk.

2 Roll out some dough and cut out several leaves at once with a pastry cutter. Mark the leaf veins with a knife.

The texture of the bark is made with a knife point.

3·To build up the foliage start at the outer edge of the crown of the tree. Moisten each leaf as it is positioned and work towards the centre of the crown. Overlap the leaves until you cover the tops of the branches.

4 The foliage is completed and three leaves are positioned halfway down the trunk.

5 Cut out the blossoms in a similar way to the leaves, but use a flower-shaped pastry cutter.

Moisten the back of each flower blossom and position on the tree. With a pointed wooden skewer, press into the centre of each flower. This will secure the blossom and give it a more natural look.

Insert a paper clip into the top of the tree for hanging.

6 Paint the trunk of the tree with burnt umber with a little black added to it. Before the paint is dry take a clean, damp paintbrush and wipe off a little of the paint to emphasize the texture. This highlights the texture of the trunk.

The blossom is then painted in white.

7 The leaves are painted in a dark green and again, before the paint is dry, take a damp paintbrush and wipe off a little paint from the ends of the leaves.

Mix a thin, light yellowy-green and brush over the ends of the leaves to highlight them.

8 When the paint is completely dry paint or spray the varnish onto the back and front.

More than one coat of varnish may be needed to seal the plaque properly.

# Step-by-step: Angel

1 Roll out a small amount of dough and cut out two wings with a moon-shaped pastry cutter.

2 Impress the pattern round the outer edge of the wings with the flat tip of a pointed knife blade. The other impressed designs are made with the outer case of an old ball-point pen and the pointed end of a cocktail stick. Place the wings so that the bottom tips overlap. Moisten them with a damp paintbrush before pressing together gently.

Make a small ball for the head, two rolls for the legs and one roll for the arms. Moisten with a damp paintbrush and put them together.

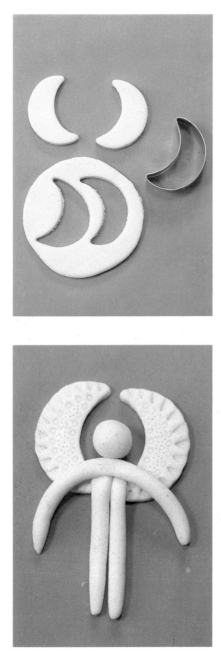

3 Roll out a small amount of dough for the bodice. Cut into a rectangle. Cut out half circles for the neck and armholes. Moisten the upper body and place the bodice in position. Tuck in the dough around the top of the shoulders and the body and under the arms. This can be done with either a modelling tool or a small knife.

For the skirt, roll out a small amount of dough very thinly. Cut into a rectangle. Taking the top edge between finger and thumb, gather it together to form the folds of the skirt. Moisten the waistline with a damp brush. Put the skirt in place and press gently. The sides of the skirt are carefully tucked underneath with a knife.

With the blade of a knife mark two Vs at the end of the legs to form the shoes.

Take the arm rolls, moisten the ends, and join them together.

4 The strands of hair are made by inserting a small roll of dough into a clay gun (or a garlic press) and gently pressing. Trim them off with a sharp knife. Moisten the head and gently put the hair in place.

Take some small dried flowers and push into the ends of the arms to form a bouquet. Insert a paper clip for hanging.

The model is now ready for baking at a low temperature. If preferred, the model can be baked without the flowers and they can be glued in position later.

5 Paint a very thin wash of burnt umber on the wings to emphasize the impressed detail. The wash should also be applied to the dress. Add slightly darker shades to emphasize the folds. Paint the shoes dark brown.

6 Leave the hair, face, arms and legs the natural dough colour. Paint the eyes and nostrils in black with a fine brush. Use the same brush to paint the red lips and the thin wash for the rosy cheeks.

To preserve the natural look of the whole model only a thin coating of varnish should be applied, but remember that the model must be sealed on the back as well.

# Step-by-step: Basket

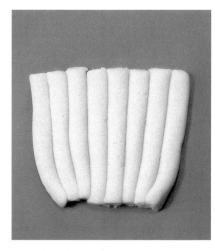  

1 To form the body of the basket take eight rolls of dough, moisten the sides and place them together.

Pinch the bottom of the rolls together to form the base of the basket.

2 Take two rolls of dough and twist them to form a rope. Moisten the bottom edge of the basket and gently press the rope against it. Trim the ends of the rope to size.

Take two rolls and form a rope to make the handle. Cut to size, moisten the ends and attach to the top edge of the basket. With a knife, cut the body of the basket to form a herring-bone pattern.

3 Roll out some dough and cut out seven leaf shapes. Using a knife, mark the veins.

Moisten the leaves and gently press them onto the top edge of the basket and around the handle.

4 To make each rose, take several small balls of dough and flatten them between finger and thumb until they are very thin.

Take the first of these flattened balls and roll it up like a Swiss roll. Take the next flattened ball and overlap the edge of the first petal. Wrap it around loosely, holding it between finger and thumb at the base.

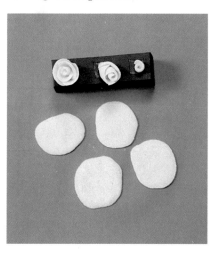

Add each subsequent petal in the same way to build up the rose shape.

Make enough roses to fill the basket. In this example there are twelve roses.

5 Moisten the ends of the roses with a damp paintbrush. Start at the front of the basket and build up the bouquet. Place the roses above each other until the basket is full. To avoid crushing the roses when they are positioned, gently push a cocktail stick into the centre to hold it while it is fixed into position. Push a paper clip into the handle for hanging or attach a ribbon to the handle after baking.

6 After baking, paint a thin wash of burnt sienna on the roses. Paint the basket and handle with a mixture of burnt sienna and a touch of black.

Before the paint is dry wipe the basket and handle with a damp brush to remove some of the colour and expose the natural dough colour underneath. This highlights the pattern of the basket and handle and also gives it a rustic appearance.

7 Finally, paint the leaves in a soft dark green. Before the paint is dry wipe the leaves with a damp paintbrush to remove some of the paint. Paint a lighter shade of green on top of these areas to highlight the leaves and give them a realistic appearance.

Spray or paint the varnish on the back and front. The rustic appearance is preserved if only one coat of varnish is used because this will avoid a glossy look.

# Step-by step: Clown

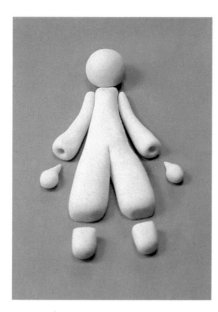

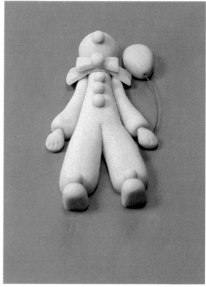

1 For the body, make a roll of dough which is thinner at one end. Take a knife and cut halfway along the roll from the thicker end.

Twist the legs so that the flat cut surface is facing downwards.

Make two more tapered rolls for the arms. Moisten the tapered ends of the arms with a damp paintbrush and attach them to the side of the body.

Make a ball of dough for the head. Moisten it with a brush and attach it to the body.

Use two small balls for the hands, and pinch them into pear shapes. Make holes in the end of the arms with a pointed wooden skewer.

Make a small roll with rounded ends and cut it in half to form the feet.

2 Form a flattened oval ball of dough for the balloon. Use small balls of dough for the buttons, shoe pompons, nose and bow tie.

Roll out a small amount of dough and cut out two bow ties, one smaller than the other. With a damp paintbrush moisten the holes in the sleeves and insert the hands.

Take the two pieces of dough formed for the shoes. Moisten the ends of the trousers and, with the cut sides facing downwards, attach the shoes to the ends of the trousers.

3 Moisten two small balls of dough and attach one to the top of each shoe.

Attach one small ball to the head to form the nose, and three more balls for buttons down the body.

Take the larger bow tie shape and moisten it with a damp paintbrush and attach it to the neck. Moisten the smaller bow tie and place it on top of the larger. Finish it off with a small ball of dough.

Stick one end of a piece of thin galvanized wire into the end of the balloon and the other end of the wire into the hand. Moisten the end of the bow tie and attach the balloon to it.

Mark the fingers on the hand with a knife.

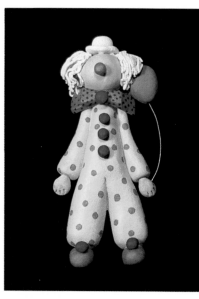

6 Emerald green spots complete the suit and the same colour is repeated on the balloon. A colour-coordinated clown!

Paint smaller bright blue spots on the bow tie.

The hair is painted a bright ginger colour, which is a mixture of burnt sienna and orange.

The figure is topped with a bright blue hat.

Finally, the eyes and mouth are painted and then outlined in black.

4 With a clay gun (or garlic press) make some dough spaghetti for the hair. Attach to each side of the head, leaving a bald patch on top.

Make two balls of dough. Flatten one and attach it to the other to form the hat. Moisten the bald patch and attach the hat.

Insert a paper clip into the hat for hanging. The model is now ready for baking.

5 The clown looks best in primary colours, so paint the suit in a bright yellow and the bow tie in a bright red.

Paint the clown's face and hands in a flesh colour. This is made by adding white to burnt sienna. Paint the buttons and pompons bright blue, and the nose red.

7 The clown is finished off with a coat of varnish on both sides.

This makes an ideal gift for a small child to hang on their bedroom wall.

# Step-by-step:Fruit Garland

1 Take two rolls of dough and twist them to form a rope. Make the rope into a circle by moistening the ends and joining them together.

2 Roll out a small amount of dough. Using pastry cutters, cut out two large leaves and five small leaves. Mark the veins with a knife.

3 With a moist paintbrush, dampen the join in the circle. Place a large leaf on each side and overlap the five smaller leaves in the centre to form a rosette.

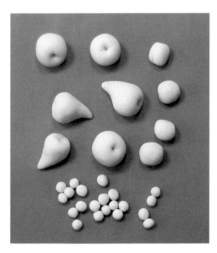

4 Make several small balls of dough for the fruit. Vary the sizes.

For the apples, take a ball of dough and cover it with a small piece of cling film (or thin polythene). Gently press a wooden skewer into the dough. Do not pierce the cling film. The creases formed by pushing in the skewer give the fruit a more natural appearance.

The pears are made by pinching one end of the ball of dough and rolling it between finger and thumb. Turn the pointed end over slightly to give a natural look. Again, cover the pear with the cling film and press in the wooden skewer.

For the plums, use the cling film but insert the skewer at the top and the bottom. Join the indentations together by gently pressing a knife blade down one side.

Use very small balls of dough to form the grapes.

5 Moisten the leaves where the fruit are to be positioned. Arrange the largest fruits first. Fill in the gaps with smaller fruits.

Finally, add the smaller balls of dough to form the bunches of grapes.

Pierce the top of the garland with a large drinking straw. A ribbon or cord can later be threaded through this for hanging.

This is now ready for baking.

6 Mix a wash with burnt umber and a little black. Paint onto the rope twist. Wipe off with a damp paintbrush to give a rustic look.

Paint the pears a light olive green, and before the paint dries wipe away some of the paint to give the highlights.

Paint the highlights over with a slight rosy colour to give the fruit a ripe appearance.

7 Paint the apples with crimson red. The highlights are again made by wiping off the paint with a clean, damp paintbrush. The highlights are then painted with a little yellow.

9 The leaves are painted with a dark green and before the paint dries the edges are wiped with a damp brush to highlight the veins.

A little yellowish-green is added to the highlights to give a realistic look.

8 Paint the plums with a mixture of permanent rose and ultramarine. The grapes are painted with a similar mixture, but more blue is added. Again, before the paint dries, wipe with a clean, damp brush to produce the highlights.

10 Spray or paint with varnish on both sides. Additional coats of varnish may be added to the fruit to give a higher degree of gloss and to contrast them with the rope twist.

Thread a ribbon or cord through the holes at the top for hanging.

This makes an attractive gift. Alternatively, keep it for yourself and show it off to your friends!

# Gallery

The following pages are filled with ideas for you to copy or adapt so that you can develop you own individual style.

Whatever you do, remember that the most important thing is to have fun doing it!

# Birds, Fish & Animals

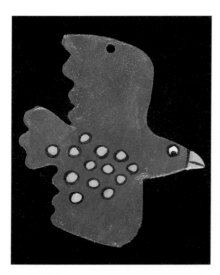

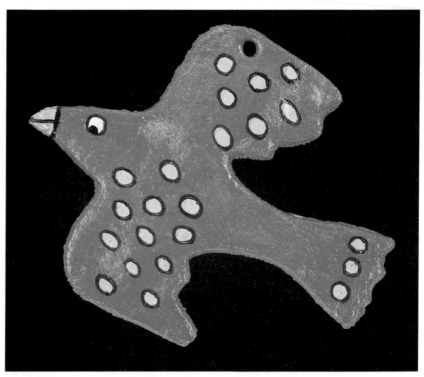

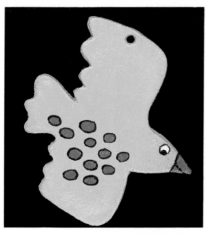

These simple, flat bird shapes have been painted on both sides so that they can be hung individually or together to make an attractive mobile. (BP)

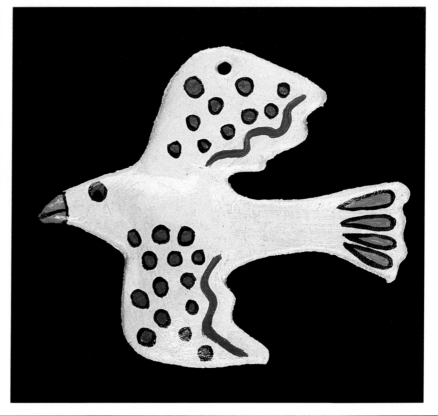

The bodies of the fat, spotty chucks are made with balls of dough which have been flattened and pinched on one side to form the tail and on the other side to form the head and beak. The beak is snipped open with a pair of scissors.

The combs are made with a flower-shaped pastry cutter. The flower shape is then cut in half, moistened and stuck on top of the head. The wattles are two tear-shaped pieces stuck underneath.

The feet are small rolls of dough which are bunched together. The neck feathers were snipped with a pair of scissors. (BP)

The teddy and the capital letter A against which he is leaning are mostly made from rolls of dough. Balls of dough are used for teddy's head, body and ears.

Alphabet teddies make excellent gifts for children, and a whole name can be made up by joining the letters together. (DC)

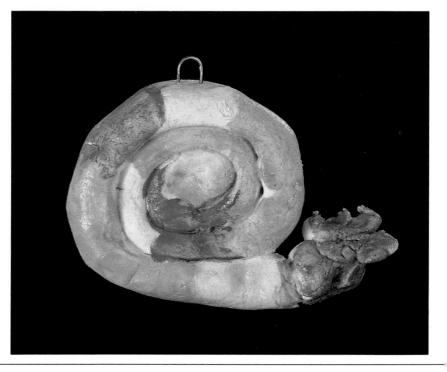

This snail was made by a ten-year old and is definitely a non-edible variety.

A coil of dough is made into a Swiss roll shape and the end pinched to form the head. (SB)

Like the birds on page 30, these simple flat shapes are easy to make.

Display them individually or as a mobile.

Tropical fish provide lots of inspiration for vibrant colour schemes. (BP)

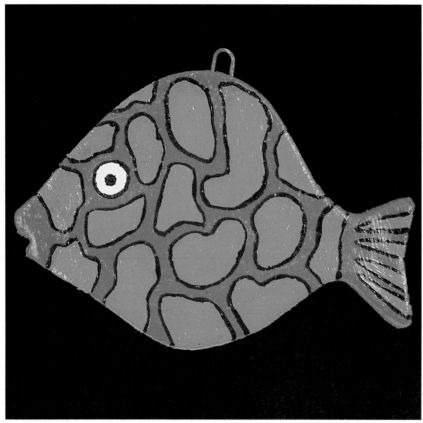

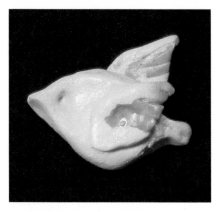

This bird on the wing, also made by a ten-year old, is wonderfully animated. (AC)

33

The handsome cockerel opposite was made from two balls of dough, one for the body and one for the head. Two rolls of dough were used for the legs.

Individual pieces of dough were made into feather shapes and built up to form the main body. They were overlapped to make it look more natural.

The base was finished off with grass which was made with a clay gun. (BP)

The base of this plaque was rolled out and cut into an arched window shape. Rolls of dough were used to form the frame and the tree branches.

After the two owl shapes were formed, the beak and feathers were snipped with a pair of scissors. The edge of a drinking straw was used to impress the upper wing feathers.

The eyes were made with the case of a ball-point pen.

The texture of the branches was scratched with the tip of a knife blade.

This worried looking sheep was largely made with the help of a garlic press. Full instructions are given on pages 16 and 17.

It is a witty example of a young teenager's first attempt at dough modelling. (EB)

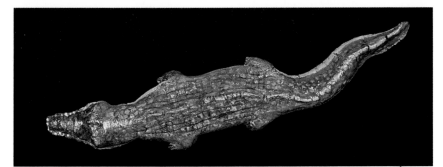

The crocodile was formed out of one long roll of dough which was squeezed into shape before the legs were added. The realistic crocodile skin effect was made with a knife.

This is a first attempt at dough modelling by a mature student. (MP)

This saddle-backed pig is made from a slightly flattened ball of dough, pinched at one end to form the snout. The snout is pushed up to form creases and these are emphasized with a knife blade. The mouth is snipped with a pair of scissors.

The legs are four rolls of dough, snipped at the end to form the trotters.

The ears were made with a leaf-shaped pastry cutter, and the tail with a garlic press. (BP)

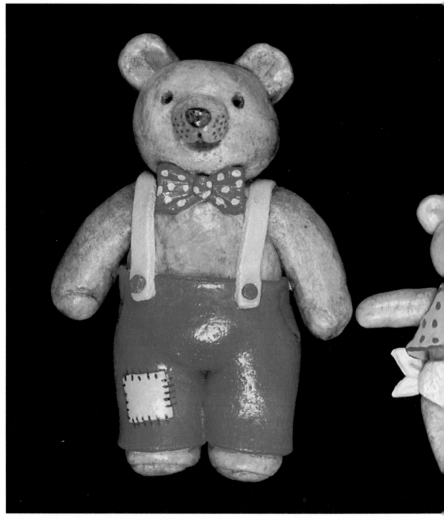

The body shape of this cow was cut from rolled out dough. The head was then cut out and stuck on the body.

A circle of dough was cut for the nose, and ears and horns were added.

The flat side of a knife blade was pressed onto the legs in order to give the impression that one leg was in front of the other. (BP)

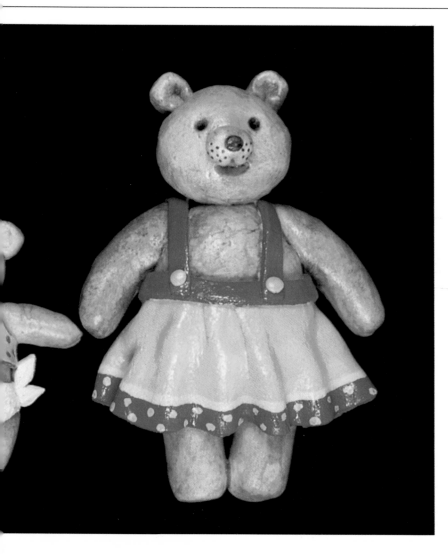

The bodies of the teddy bears and their heads were formed with balls of clay. Rolls of clay were added for the legs and arms. Small balls of dough were added for the muzzle, nose and ears.

The clothes were made from thinly rolled dough which was cut to shape and moulded around the bodies.

The bears were given more character by adding painted details such as borders on the skirt and the patch on the trousers. (BP)

The body of this performing seal is made from a fat sausage shape, pinched at one end to form the head.

Flat pieces of dough are stuck on to form the tail and flippers, and then marked with a knife.

The coloured ball is held on the seal's nose by pushing a cocktail stick into the ball and then through the head and neck. (BP)

# Monsters

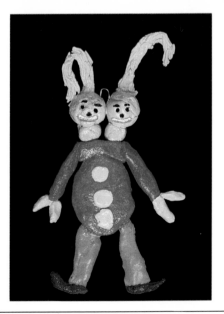

This jolly octopus was made with thickly rolled dough which had been cut into a rectangle.

The top corners of the rectangle were trimmed to form the head shape. The remaining part of the rectangle was cut with a knife into eight tentacles which were pinched to a point at their bottom ends. They were then spread out and curled up. (BP)

This gruesome two-headed monster came from the imagination of a ten-year old. (CB)

The body of this dragon was made from a fat tapered coil which was pinched up to form a ridge along its back. V-shapes were cut out of the ridge to form the 'points' along the spine.

The legs were made from fat coils, and the feet were snipped to form three claws. Wings, ears and horns were then added.

The eyes and nostrils were small balls of dough with a pencil point pushed into them. The pencil was also used to produce the body texture. (BP)

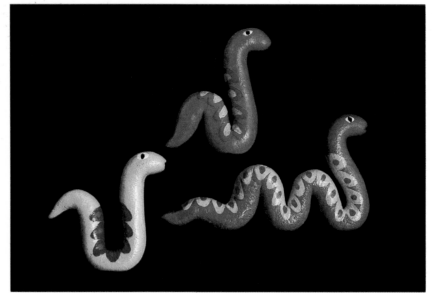

Snakes are easily made with simple rolls of dough bent to form their animated bodies.

They are dried in an upright position so that they are free-standing.

They are very easy for children to make and paint. (BP)

# Plants & Trees

The pear tree opposite is a variation on the tree shown in the Step by Step section on pages 18 and 19.

Although it looks very complicated, it is easy to make. It simply requires patience!

It makes a delightful wall plaque. (BP)

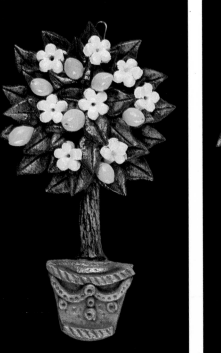

The lemon and orange trees standing in the tubs are simple variations on the tree theme.

The leaves and blossom were cut from rolled out dough with pastry cutters.

The decorations on the tubs were made of thin, flattened rolls of dough which have been impressed with a pencil point.

The texture of the oranges and lemons was made by rolling the balls of dough on a concrete path! (BP)

The lilies (top right) are a simplified version of the roses shown on page 22.

A very thin roll of dough was used for the centre of the flower. A ball of dough was pinched into a very thin circle and then wrapped around the small roll to form a petal.

The plinth is a series of thin rolls of dough. (BP)

# Garlands

An attractive gift for the bride and groom, this garland could even form part of the wedding cake decoration.

The basic horseshoe shape was made from a dough roll.

Leaves and flowers were then added down each side. The grass on which the couple are standing was pressed through a clay gun. (BP)

A special Valentine's Day gift, but here we are saying it with dough flowers. (BP)

This stylized tree with its pairs of birds has a warm rustic glow. A dough circle was first made and vertical and horizontal branches were added. These were then covered with cut out leaves. The bird shapes were drawn on card and this was cut into a template. Using the template, the bird shapes were cut from rolled dough. (BP)

Another variation on the Valentine plaque, but this time in a low relief rather than open shape.

A piece of rolled dough was cut out into a heart shape and a very thin coil added around the outside to frame it.

The leaves, flowers and bird shapes were then added, together with an impressed background made with a pointed wooden stick and a sharp knife. The whirls and curls at the top of the heart shape were made from very thin rolls of dough.

The completed plaque was first painted with burnt sienna and then cream paint was added to the relief areas. (BP)

This bird garland was made from dough rolls twisted together.

The heads and bodies are dough balls, with the head pinched to form a beak. The wings and tails are flattened dough rolls which were formed into tear shapes. Feathers were marked with a knife. The flowers and leaves were finally added and covered the joins in the twists.

A paper clip was inserted in the top for hanging. (BP)

A small amount of dough was rolled out and cut into the shape of the wheatsheaf. A knife was used to score the stalks at the base of the sheaf.

The upper part was made of thin rolls of dough which were snipped with scissors to form the ears of wheat.

A very thin roll of dough was used to form the tie around the centre of the sheaf.

The mice are tiny balls of dough which were pinched to a pear shape, and the tail and ears then added. (VS)

Pears, apples, cherries and lemons make up this garland of fruit. The base is a simple dough roll which was formed into a circle and covered in leaves. The leaves were cut out with a pastry cutter and the veins marked with a knife. The fruit was made from small balls of dough. A wash of burnt sienna was painted on, and before it was dry it was wiped with a clean, damp brush to give highlights on the fruit. The final coat of varnish gave the garland a rich, warm appearance. This garland can be used either as a wall plaque or a candle ring as a table decoration. It could also be painted in gold to make a festive Christmas decoration or even a gift. (BP)

# Fruit

This colourful cornucopia of fruit and flowers makes a striking wall decoration. (BP)

The basket below was formed from rolled dough with twisted rolls for the handle and base. A fork was used to make the basket-weave pattern.

The basket was then filled with a variety of individually made fruits including grapes and a pineapple. (BP)

My husband's first attempts at dough modelling. Proof positive that anyone can make dough models! I must confess I helped with the painting. (DP/BP)

The textured skin of these oranges was made by rolling the balls of dough on a concrete footpath, which added greatly to their realistic appearance. (BP)

Fruit is a good subject for salt dough, and it can be made into plaques of individual fruits or mixed fruits.

These can also look very attractive when mounted in frames.

The branch of cherries was made from three rolls of dough which were scored with a knife blade to produce the texture of the bark. The cherries were made from individual balls of dough with fine galvanized wire pushed into them to form the stalks. The stalks were then pushed into the branches.

Leaf shapes were then cut out and pressed gently in place over the joins of the wire and branches.

The ripe pears were assembled by first cutting the leaf shapes and grouping them together. Each pear was made from a ball of dough which was pinched between thumb and finger to elongate it. A wooden pointed skewer was then inserted into the base of each

pear using the cling film technique described on page 26. The stalks were made from short pieces of cocktail sticks.

The pears were painted in olive green, with burnt sienna and crimson for the highlights.

The apples plaque was formed in a similar way to the pairs.

Leaves were laid down first and then balls of dough for the apples. They were painted in crimson and highlighted with a warm yellow. Then, with a fine brush, streaks of crimson were painted across the highlights.

The characteristic crease down the peaches is made by

Individual blackberries were made by first pushing a cocktail stick into a small ball of dough. The cocktail stick was used as a support while tiny individual balls of dough were stuck on the larger central ball. The resulting finished blackberry was then gently slid off the stick and positioned on the garland.

The flowers were cut out with a pastry cutter. The back of each flower was moistened and positioned on the garland then finally secured by pressing a pointed wooden skewer into the centre of each flower. (BP)

This rustic horn of plenty was made by cutting a horn shape from some rolled out dough and then marking the basket-weave effect with a fork.

The end of the horn was covered with flowers, leaves, fruit and berries. Two small rolls of dough were twisted together to form the handle and attached to the horn with a small dough loop. (BP)

covering the ball of dough with cling film and impressing a knife blade from top to bottom. The cling film prevents the knife from cutting into the dough and the final result is a slightly rounded crease on the dough's surface. The succulent appearance of the peaches was achieved with a mixture of burnt sienna, crimson and white. Highlights were painted in a pale yellow. (BP)

Blackberry fruits and flowers make up this unusual garland. Two twisted rolls of dough were used to form the rope base.

# Baskets

A small cane basket was used as a mould for this basket of fruit.

A small amount of dough was rolled out and then gently pressed into the cane basket. The surplus was trimmed off.

Two small rolls of dough were twisted into a rope. The trimmed edge of the basket was moistened and the rope laid on top. The surplus was cut off and the ends joined together.

The handle was made from a flattened roll of stiff dough (to hold its shape) with an impressed design on it.

The basket was air dried for several days. This caused the dough to contract and it was then easily removed from its mould. It was baked in the normal way.

The strawberries were balls of dough pinched to a point, and the surface texture was added with a pointed skewer.

The leaves were made with a star-shaped cutter and stuck to the tops of the strawberries by gently pressing them with the end of the skewer. (BP)

A small ceramic bowl was used as a mould for this basket of summer fruit.

The bowl was lightly oiled and strips of dough laid in it. The top was trimmed, moistened and a small dough rope was pressed gently across the trimmed edge. The dough contracted during baking and the basket was then easily removed from the ceramic mould. (BP)

This basket of delicate roses has been painted with a light wash to complement the natural colour of the dough. (BP)

This tiny basket was moulded in a ceramic cup using the same method as the summer fruit basket shown opposite.

Three ropes make up the plaited handle, and tiny balls of dough were stuck around larger balls of dough to form the berries. (BP)

Overflowing with an abundance of fruit and berries, this basket is perfect for a country kitchen.

It was first painted with a light wash made from burnt sienna. A little black was then painted on to emphasize the texture and decoration of the basket and fruit. (BP)

# Circus

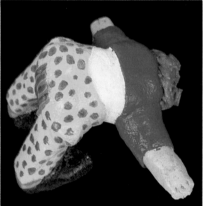

Caught in the act of attempting a head stand, this clown was made from four rolls of dough for the arms and legs and a fatter roll for the body.

The trousers and sweater were shaped from thinly rolled dough and carefully placed in position.

His hair was made with a clay gun, although a garlic press could also have been used.

The model was allowed to air dry before baking and was prevented from collapsing by supporting the body with a piece of oblong cardboard which had been folded into a V-shape and placed under the body. (RS)

This clown was made from two long rolls of dough which form the legs and go right up to the shoulders. Another dough roll was laid across for the arms.

The shirt was made from thinly rolled dough and placed over the arms and body. Head and trousers were then added.

The arms were bent at the elbows so that the hands touched the trousers. Patch pockets were cut out and fixed on to cover the hands.

The model was finished off with two balls of dough for the feet and then the braces and the bow tie were added. (VS)

Full instructions for making the clown opposite can be found on pages 24 and 25.

The entrance of the clowns is heralded by this enthusiastic drummer with large red cheeks.

The drum was made with a ball of dough which was flattened at top and bottom to form the sides of the drum. It was attached to the body and then a very thin roll of dough was used to make the strap around the drummer's neck.

The drumsticks are small balls of dough attached to pieces of cocktail sticks which have been pushed into the hands.

His mop of hair has been 'roughed up' with a fork. (RS)

Madame Rosie prepares to reveal the future as she gazes into the all-seeing dough-ball!

The figure was made from dough rolls, with a ball of dough for the head.

The gaily painted dress, curtains and tablecloth were made from very thinly rolled dough so that it could easily be folded for the frills and flounces. (RS)

The body of the ballet dancer is made with dough rolls.

Her tutu was formed by rolling out the dough very thinly and pleating it into ruffles around the waist. (RS)

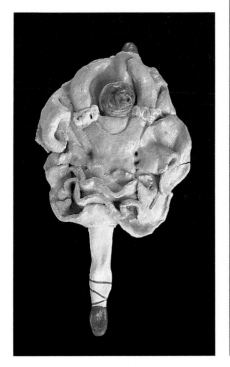

The spirit of the Moulin Rouge lives on with these two naughty can-can dancers. The figures are crowned with bright ginger hair which was made with the aid of a garlic press. The ample bosoms are formed from dough rolls enhanced by the plunging necklines of the dresses made from thinly rolled dough. The painted black garters add the finishing touch. (RS)

These two young children are enjoying themselves in a brightly painted fairground swing.

Rolled out dough was cut to the shape of the swingboat. Thin rolls of dough were used to decorate the sides, which were later painted in vibrant colours.

The small figures have expressive faces with button noses made from tiny balls of dough. The eyes and mouth were made with the ends of cocktail sticks.

Holes were made in the base of the swingboat and through the children's hands. The hanging cord was then threaded through.

This is ideal for a child's bedroom. (BP)

The body of the circus strong man, knees buckling from the weight of the barbells, was made from dough rolls. His hair and moustache are dough strands made with a clay gun. The barbells are simply a cocktail stick with balls of dough on each end. (BP)

This energetic lady helps keep trim by dancing away her excess weight. With the addition of some string she can also become a trapeze artist. (RS)

The brightly coloured balloons were made from small balls of dough which were pinched into pear shapes. Pieces of galvanized wire are used to attach them to the boy's hand. (BP)

# Figures

The upright piano is a slab of rolled dough.

The figure is made from dough rolls clothed in very thinly rolled dough.

The music, keyboard and pianist's collar are all made from paper. (VS)

The dynamic duo opposite are lost in musical reverie. Their intense concentration is shown by their closed eyes.

Cocktail sticks are used for their bows and the necks of the violin and cello. (RS)

A somewhat distraught conductor leaps into action. The tails of his impressive coat are made from thinly rolled dough, and his baton is made from a matchstick. The very expressive face is painted with a fine brush, as are the spots on his tie. (RS)

Standing to attention, this guardsman is clad in a smart red tunic and impressive bearskin.

His rifle is formed around a cocktail stick which has been pressed through his hand. (RS)

This bloated business man is 'Mr Big' in every sense. He was made from a fat roll of dough which was cut up the middle to form his legs.

His city uniform of elegant grey waistcoat and black jacket is made from thinly rolled dough.

The figure is completed with a cocktail stick cigar. (BP)

This sporty roadster would make an ideal gift for Father's Day. The features of the driver could be a caricature of the recipient! (RS)

The intrepid fireman wrestles with a red hose. He cuts a very dashing figure with bright yellow trousers and black tunic, topped with a yellow helmet. (RS)

The long arm, or in this case, the long legs of the Law may yet catch up with the sporty roadster.
    This is a beautifully animated model, with the uniform made from thinly rolled dough. The silver helmet badge and sergeant's stripes are finely painted details. (RS)

The two sepia period pieces opposite are pleasantly nostalgic. The bustling appearance of the mother is emphasized by the flowing coat and skirt, which were made from thinly rolled dough.

Sitting on a rustic garden seat, the elegantly dressed twins are engrossed in their books.

The hems of their skirts are pinched to make them very thin. The untrimmed edge then looks as if it has a scalloped

appearance. The sunhats are simply circles of dough into which a finger has been pushed to create the crown. They have been trimmed with tiny roses. (VS, BP)

A wonderfully active sailor dances the hornpipe. His shirt and bellbottoms were made from thinly rolled dough which was wrapped around the dough roll body and legs.

His hat is trimmed with a fine black dough ribbon. (RS)

A most impressive fisherman dressed for action in sou'wester and thigh boots. His catch includes two fish and a crab. The very effective fishing net previously contained oranges! (VS)

Dressed in her Sunday best, this young lady with long dark hair made from dough strands (pressed through a clay gun) is waiting to meet her beau.

Her large picture hat is trimmed with a bow and roses.

Her pretty face has delicately painted features and the dress and pinafore have finely painted detail in sepia tones. (BP)

This is the beau of the adjacent young lady. He is smartly dressed in pin-stripe trousers and spotted neckerchief.

He is also sporting a dashing moustache made with the aid of a clay gun.

His ensemble is completed with his brown Derby hat. (BP)

This beautifully formed couple have just taken their wedding vows. The bride's dress is especially fine with lace hem and collar pierced with a cocktail stick.

The flower bouquet is glued on after the model has been baked.

The groom is smartly dressed in check trousers and plain jacket.

Both figures have neatly painted features. (VS)

The advancing years have brought grandmother and grandfather closer together.

He has his pipe with stem made from a cocktail stick, and she has her knitting with the needles made from cocktail sticks.

Notice the fine detail, which extends to the buttons and his eyebrows. (VS)

This expressive model captures the local darts champion in mid-throw.

Most of this model was made with flattened dough rolls. The T-shirt is thinly rolled dough which does not quite cover his beer belly. (RS)

This animated rugby player leaps to catch the ball. Notice the accurate detail of the shirt, socks and even the muddy limbs. (RS)

Well padded for action, this American Football player looks quite menacing.

The details of the leggings, shirt and helmet have been painted with a fine brush. (RS)

This inventive model has some nice details. The top and legs of the snooker table are made from rolls of dough. Balls of dough have been added under the top and cross-hatch painted to simulate net pockets.

The cue is made from a cocktail stick. The glass tankard was made by pressing the blunt end of a wooden pencil into a small ball of dough and forming it around the end. A small roll was added for the handle. (RS)

The cricketer's hands were made from rolled dough which was attached to the legs and marked with a knife blade. The ribs on the sweater were also marked with a knife blade.

The figure is completed with finely painted detail on the face and sweater. (RS)

Inspired by the work of the artist Beryl Cook, this energetic lady is attempting to dance away her excess weight.

A fat roll of dough was used to form the torso. Tapering rolls of dough were used to form the legs and arms to emphasize the plumpness of the figure.

The head was made from a ball of dough and the bosom from two smaller ones.

Her leotard was shaped from thinly rolled out dough and carefully placed over the body. Thin rolls of dough were also used for the headband and leg warmers.

The delicate pink flesh tones complete the model. (RS)

The sunworshipper's airbed was made from rolled out dough, cut to shape.

The figure was formed from rolls of dough which were shaped to form the muscles.

The straw hat was made from two circles of dough which have been joined together.

The towel was made from thinly rolled dough which was wrinkled and folded to give a natural shape. This was emphasized by the blue painted lines. (RS)

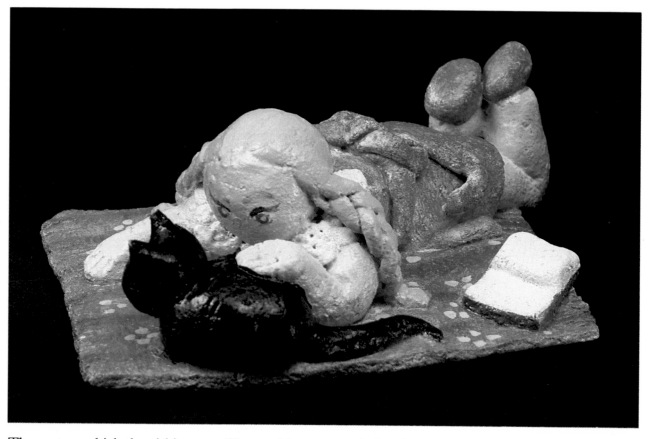

The mat on which the girl is lying was cut from rolled out dough. The girl's body, arms and legs are dough rolls and a dough ball is used for the head. Smaller dough balls are used for the feet. The fingers have been marked with a knife blade.

The hair was made from very thin rolls of plaited dough and attached to each side of the head.

The dress was cut out from thinly rolled dough, as was the collar which was pierced with a pointed stick to give the appearance of lace.

The cat was made from two balls of dough, one of which was pinched to form the ears. (RS)

The pool base was a circle of dough and its sides were made from a roll of dough. The base was then roughened to give the appearance of water.

A roll of dough was used for the body, with thinner rolls for the arms and legs. These were cut and positioned on the base to give the impression that the body was submerged under the water.

The toes were snipped with scissors and a ball of dough added for the head. This was topped with strands of clay from a clay gun. They were bunched on top to give the impression of a pony tail. (RS)

# Weddings

The bodies of the choir boys are made from rolled out dough cut to the shape of their surplices. Balls of dough were added for the heads and feet.

The arms are slightly flattened tapered rolls of dough. Pieces of cocktail sticks were pushed into the ends and balls of dough pushed on to form the hands.

The collars are thinly rolled dough which has been folded, flounced and placed around the neckline. Impressed detail was added to the surplices to give the appearance of lace.

Their expressively open mouths were made with the end of a wooden skewer. (RS)

Two balls of dough were used to form the cherub's head and body. Three rolls were used to make the arms and the one visible leg. The leg was attached to the body and thinly rolled

dough was then attached to form the gown.

More thinly rolled dough was wrapped around the arms to form the sleeves. They were attached to the body and smoothed with a damp brush. Thin ribbons of dough were attached to the hem cuffs and neck to form the frills. The hands and feet were made from balls of dough. The hands were brought up towards the mouth so that the cherub appeared to be sucking his thumb. The fingers were marked with a knife blade. The toes are tiny balls of dough. A small ball of dough was used for the nose and a slightly bigger one for the ear. Wing shapes were cut out of rolled dough, attached to the back and marked with a knife to suggest feathers. The hair was made with a clay gun. After baking, the limbs, head and body were painted with acrylic paint. The wings were painted with Humbrol gold metallic paint but left unvarnished to prevent them from becoming dulled. (BP)

This elegant bridal couple have beautiful painted features. The lacy edge of the dress was made by cutting it with dressmaker's pinking shears (or a pastry cutter can be used).

Tiny holes were impressed into the hem of the dress with a cocktail stick to give the impression of lace.

After varnishing, the finishing touches are the bride's bouquet and the groom's buttonhole, both using dried flowers. (VS)

# Christmas

The snowman's body was formed over an upturned dariole mould which had first been oiled. The mould was then covered with rolled out dough. The head is a ball of dough and the arms are two small rolls. Another ball was made into a hat. The broom handle is a cocktail stick. (BP)
wreath was made in a similar way to the holly wreath opposite. (BP)

Miniature garlands look very attractive when hung on either doors or walls. This pretty little

Christmas trees require a little care but are very simple and quick for both adults and children to make.

The outline of the tree was first drawn on baking paper and the shape was then filled with dough strands (made with a clay gun). The points of the tree were gently pushed into shape with a knife blade.

The decorations are simply balls of dough.

The tree was first painted in a dark green and then highlights were added in a lighter green. Bright colours are best for the decorations, although metallic colours can look very effective. (BP)

This colourful garland is an ideal Christmas decoration for children to make. A dough roll was formed into a circle and dough strands loosely stuck to it.

The holly leaves were cut out with pastry cutters. Small balls of dough were then stuck on to form the berries. The bow was made from strips of dough, but the alternative is to add a ribbon bow after the model has been painted. Do not forget the paper clip for hanging. (BP)

The wings of this Christmas Angel were made from small rolls of dough laid side by side. A herring-bone pattern was impressed with a sharp knife.

The smaller feathers are small, flattened balls of dough placed on top of the rolls and overlapped.

A small circle of dough was cut out for the halo. The body and wings were placed on top of the halo and pressed in position. The wings were painted with gold Humbrol paint. (BP)

This festive swag was made by starting at the base and overlapping leaves, flowers and twisted rolls. It was finished off with a large dough bow. After baking, the model was painted all over with dark brown acrylic paint. This was then varnished. A medium flat brush was then used to highlight the details with Humbrol gold paint. (BP)

This angel was also painted in dark brown acryllic paint, varnished and then highlighted with Humbrol gold paint. (BP)

This simple garland was made from twisted dough rolls. The leaves were cut with a pastry cutter. The berries were small balls of dough impressed with a small wooden skewer. (BP)

This swag was made from plaited dough rolls covered with ivy leaves (made with a pastry cutter). Large leaves and berries cover the cut ends of the plait.

After painting and varnishing it was finished with a pleated paper bow. (BP)

This festive bow can be hung above a wall light or picture. (BP)

This candle holder was made from a garland of holly leaves, berries and bows.

The candle ring was made with a roll of dough formed into a circle. It was supported on the base of an oiled ceramic egg cup so that the leaves could hang down while they were being baked. Small berries were attached between the leaves.

A garland of twisted dough rolls makes up the base for this triple candle holder. The three groups of leaves were then added to the garland.

Three pairs of dough circles were snipped with scissors to produce petal shapes. Two of these were then placed on each of the groups of leaves. The petals were folded upwards so that they would hold the candles in place.